TO ADAM AND LUKA, MY SUNSHINE EVERY DAY.

Published by
North Atlantic Books
Berkeley, California

Cover art by John Bajet
Book design by Happenstance Type-O-Rama

Printed in Canada

Morning, Sunshine! is sponsored and published by the Society for the Study of Native Arts and Sciences (dba North Atlantic Books), an educational nonprofit based in Berkeley, California, that collaborates with partners to develop cross-cultural perspectives, nurture holistic views of art, science, the humanities, and healing, and seed personal and global transformation by publishing work on the relationship of body, spirit, and nature.

North Atlantic Books' publications are available through most bookstores. For further information, visit our website at www.northatlanticbooks.com or call 800-733-3000.

Library of Congress Cataloguing-in-Publication data is available from the publisher upon request.

Printed and bound in Canada by Friesens, January 2020. Job #262249

1 2 3 4 5 6 7 8 9 Friesens 25 24 23 22 21 20

North Atlantic Books is committed to the protection of our environment. We print on recycled paper whenever possible and partner with printers who strive to use environmentally responsible practices.

MORNING, SUNSHINE!

Keely Parrack

Illustrated by

John Bajet

North Atlantic Books
Berkeley, California

Bird song fills the air,
harmonies and melodies
welcome in the dawn.

At dawn, it is not yet light enough for songbirds to **forage**, but it is dark enough to hide from most **predators**, making it the perfect time to sing out loud and clear. Some birds sing, "Come here! I'm still alive, strong and available," hoping to attract a mate. Others are singing, "Go away, this is my perch," defending their **territory**. Some female songbirds go from tree to tree, listening to the songs before choosing a mate. Some male songbirds can sing over 1,000 songs!

Startled moths flutter, searching for safe places to rest before sunrise.

Most moths are **nocturnal**. Some eat **nectar** from night flowering plants, some don't eat at all, but many creatures like to eat them. Moths are sometimes **camouflaged** to look like tree bark or **lichen**. Other types of moth have markings that warn potential **predators** away, such as wings that look like huge bird eyes or tails that look like snake heads. Some moths even mimic or act like other creatures, such as spiders or wasps, to try to stop themselves from being eaten.

Pop up, quiver ears,
cottontails skitter scatter,
leaping with delight!

Rabbits have big ears and eyes to help warn them when **predators** are nearby. They can see 360 degrees around themselves—in front, at their sides, and back—except for a tiny blind spot in front of their nose. They can swivel their ears separately to hear sounds up to 2 miles away, in two different directions at the same time! When rabbits are happy, they jump and twist in the air. This is called a **binky**—both pet and wild rabbits do this!

Silver paths crisscross,
snails and slugs slither away,
seeking damp spaces.

Snail and slug trails are made of **mucus**. This helps them to stay moist and protects them from the sun's heat and from being harmed by any sharp objects they might slide over. It also acts like a glue that helps them stick to things they want to climb, like walls, plant stems, and flowerpots. The mucus is so sticky that snails and slugs can even travel upside down. In the early morning, snail and slug tracks leave silver, windy paths!

A flock of crows takes
to the sky, black capes flapping,
beaks caw-caw-cawing.

Crows are very **social**. They **roost** together, share the best places to find food, and teach each other new tricks, such as smashing open walnut shells by dropping them onto roofs. Crows are so smart they can recognize peoples' faces, especially ones that have been mean or kind to them. They share this information with other crows. A family of crows can have as many as fifteen individuals, so that flock of roosting crows may well be one big happy family!

Silent in shadow,
a shy-footed, flick-tailed deer
steps into morning.

Most deer have coats that change color with the seasons. This helps them stay camouflaged in their habitats. Baby deer, or fawns, are born with no smell, so predators can't sniff them out! Deer turn each ear separately to help them hear the tiniest movements. This helps them hide or run from danger. Scientists believe deer may be able to see ultraviolet light. This makes it easier for them to see at twilight and may be why deer are crepuscular, most active at dawn and dusk.

Tiny hummingbird
hovers in the orange tree,
sipping sweet blossoms.

The ruby-throated hummingbird is so small it weighs less than a nickel. Their eggs are about the size of a jellybean. Hummingbirds beat their wings between 12 to 90 times a second, to hover in place, and between 50 to 200 times a second to fly like helicopters: up, down, forward, or even backward. They are the only birds that can fly backward! They have great eyesight but almost no sense of smell, so they can see the delicious orange blossoms but can't enjoy their scent!

Black beetle scurries
between plant pots and pebbles,
racing for the leaves.

Beetles are one of the largest groups of living creatures on Earth. One in every five living organisms is a beetle. They tend to be **nocturnal**, eating at night and hiding in the daytime. Some are pests, but others are helpful **pest controllers**, eating slugs, caterpillars, and other small bugs. The smallest beetle is 1 millimeter long, about the size of a pencil tip. The largest is 20 centimeters, longer than a pencil. **Fossil evidence** proves that beetles have been around for over 250 million years!

A dumpling robin
hops along the garden fence,
on his matchstick legs.

Robin legs may be skinny, but they have strong muscles designed for hopping and running. They also use their medium-length tails to balance their fluffy red chests. American robins are part of the thrush family and are one of the few species of song-birds that can both run and hop. Hopping from branch to branch takes little **energy,** but hopping around on the ground takes lots of energy, which makes some **ornithologists** believe robins sometimes hop just for fun!

Shimmer dew drops cling
to strands of silk perfection,
spider lies in wait.

Spider silk starts off as a liquid stored in the spider's **abdomen**. This hardens to form a silk thread as soon as it is released from the **spinnerets: organs** underneath the abdomen. Each spinneret produces a different type of silk. Common garden or orb spiders make up to seven types of silk—from sticky to trap insects, elastic to keep the web from breaking, and strong anchor threads that hold the web in place. Some spiders' silk, weight-for-weight, is stronger than steel. Most garden spiders repair or replace their webs every day. Sometimes they recycle their old web first by eating it!

A faint blush of light
spreads across the horizon,
painting puff-clouds pink.

Sunlight is made from different colored light waves. The shortest waves are cooler colors, like blues and greens. The longest ones are hotter colors, like reds and yellows. Light waves are scattered by tiny particles in our atmosphere, such as dust and water droplets. In the daytime, when the sun is higher in the sky, there is less atmosphere between us and the sun, so the cooler, shorter light waves make the sky look blue. But at twilight, when the sun is low on the horizon, the amount of air between us and the sun increases. The shorter light waves scatter away, leaving the longer light waves behind. These hotter colored waves are reflected in the sky, turning the clouds pink!

A murmur of bees
clinging to the lemon grove,
hum for their breakfast.

The honeybees' hum comes from the vibration of their wings, which can stroke up to 200 beats a second. A honeybee may visit between 50-100 flowers while out collecting **pollen**, before flying the 2 to 3 miles home to her hive, where it will be made into honey. A single honeybee makes only 1/12th of a teaspoon of honey in her lifetime. That's probably why each hive contains between 20,000-80,000 bees!

Hungry in their nest,
fluffy dove chicks wriggle and
cry out to be fed.

Dove chicks drink pigeon milk, made by their dove parents, for the first few days of their life. They drink it by sticking their heads into their parents' wide-open mouths. Both parents make it in their **crops**, a sack-like food container near their throats. This milk is even richer in **protein** and fat than the cows' milk we drink. The parent doves will carry on feeding the **nestlings** with seeds for another 2 weeks. After that, the chicks will search for food by themselves.

Sharp nosed, bush-tailed fox,
slips beneath a garden shed
to her hungry pups.

Foxes are shy and **nocturnal**: most active from dusk to dawn. They hunt small mammals, like rats or mice, and **forage** for fruit and insects. Foxes tend to mate with the same partner for life, building dens in the wild to raise their young. Some have moved into cities and towns, finding a plentiful food supply. Foxes have **adapted** to this new **environment** by making dens under sheds, decks, or porches. They stay with their pups until they have taught them how to hunt and fend for themselves. Then, the whole family will move on.

The sunlight dazzles,
dripping gold from every tree.
Morning has begun!

As the earth rotates toward the sun, the sun appears to rise, then move across the sky, before sinking down again. This takes 24 hours, which we call a day. If you live on, or near, the **equator,** the amount of sunlight you get will be almost the same each day. But if you live further north or south, your days will get shorter in the winter and longer in the summer. We think of morning as starting when the sun appears, but in winter you may have to get up long before the sun rises, and in summer, long afterward!

GLOSSARY

abdomen: The body part that contains the digestive organs: the stomach, intestines etc.

adapt: Adjust to a new situation or environment.

atmosphere: The gasses surrounding the earth that make up our air.

binky: When rabbits leap and twist in the air with joy.

camouflage: Ability to hide by blending into the surroundings.

crepuscular: Most active at dawn and dusk.

crop: An internal pouch next to a mourning dove's throat that extends to store food, such as seeds, which later can be made into "crop" milk for the dove's nestlings.

energy: The ability to be active. Energy can be potential, or stored energy, so being saved up for future use or being actively used. We get our energy by eating food, and so do many animals and plants.

environment: The area and circumstances in which you live.

equator: The imaginary line that goes around the middle of Earth, so that the North and South Pole are equal distance away.

exhibit: Show or perform.

fawn: A baby deer.

forage: To search for food.

fossil evidence: Remains of organisms preserved in stone or trapped amber—clues for how life used to be millions of years ago.

habitat: Natural place or environment where an animal lives.

horizon: The apparent edge where the ground appears to meet the sky.

lichen: A fungus that combines symbiotically with some algae (to the benefit of both), forming crust growths on trees and rocks.

light waves: How we see visible light. Each wave has two parts: electric and magnetic, forming electromagnetic waves. We see light waves as the colors of the rainbow.

mucus: A slimy substance produced by glands or membranes for protection or lubrication.

nectar: Sweet sugary liquid made by some plants.

nestlings: Chicks (baby birds) that are too young to leave their nest.

nocturnal: Mostly active at night and asleep during the day.

organ: A body part of a living organism that has a vital function such as a heart or liver.

ornithologist: A scientist specializing in the study of birds.

pest control: The reduction of a species of life determined to be a pest, or nuisance, to our health, the environment, or the economy.

predator: An animal that naturally hunts or preys on others.

proteins: Long chains of molecules built from even smaller particles called amino acids. They are found in some foods and are an essential part of any living organism.

pollen: The male part of the flower found in the dust-like sticky grains.

roost: When birds gather to rest or sleep. Also, the name for the place they settle to rest or sleep.

scientist: A person engaged in the systematic pursuit of knowledge about the natural world in order to describe it and make predictions.

social: Likes and seeks company, living in an organized community.

spinneret: An organ in a spider, silkworm, or insect's body through which silk is produced.

territory: An area of land under the rule of a leader. In the world of nature, this refers to an area of land occupied and defended by an animal or bird (or a group of them).

twilight: The time between dawn and sunrise before it is daytime and dusk and night before it is nighttime.

ultraviolet: See also light waves. Ultraviolet means beyond violet light, which is the shortest light wave a human can see. Ultraviolet light is made of short electromagnetic waves invisible to the human eye but visible to many animals and birds.

WHAT IS HAIKU?

The poems in this book are called haiku. Haiku is a form of Japanese poetry with seventeen syllables or beats, usually in three lines. The first line has five syllables, the second seven, and the third five.

One way to find how many syllables a word has is to clap them out.

> Take your name, or mine, Keely. That would be two beats: Kee - ly.

> Try an object. Apple would be app - le. That's two beats.

> Hummingbird would be hum - ming - bird, three beats.

The first haiku were written in Japan over four hundred years ago. Traditionally haiku is about nature and seasons and does not rhyme. Today haiku are written by people all over the world about many different things.

HOW TO HAIKU

You can write haiku about anything. A good way to start is to look at the world around you. I wrote all of these haiku after watching wildlife in my backyard.

Look out of the window. What can you see, hear, smell, and feel? Birdsong? Cars? Trees? Buildings? Make a list of words or pictures. Now sort them into three lines. See if you can describe just one thing or one moment.

For example, I wrote this after watching a butterfly:

> Creamy petals float
> from blossom to sweet blossom;
> nectar for breakfast.

Or you could start with a pet or an animal you like.

Here's a list of words I made about my cat: fuzzy, fluffy, silky fur, twitching paws, rough tongue, quiet purr, hiding in the closet, snuggled on my lap, smiling.

I put them into three lines with five-seven-five syllables:

> Silky fur, fuzz face,
> Twitch paws dreaming, soft purr smile,
> Snuggled on my lap.

Once you get started, you'll see ideas for haiku everywhere!